Reinvent or Undertake

Tips to succeed in the market through a personal reinvention within a company or entrepreneurship in your own business.

Vinny Roberts

Introduction

Today, it becomes increasingly difficult to be happy in our job. We remember our parents and thought that they seemed to be happier with what they were doing or even better positioned financially. Unfortunately, it is the reality in this changing world. We can no longer settle for earning a college degree and hoping to make a fortune from it. Every day there are more professionals and fewer and fewer options to develop in.

Because I have been in that position, I decided to write this book. In our days we have two paths, we specialize, or we simply decide to start our own business. There is no third option, since that option is to spend our lives working for a company just to bring money home, no matter how bitter we may be with it.

The first step to get out of this situation is to recognize that you have a problem, that is, to accept that you are frustrated in your job. The second step is to pursue your dream, either growing within a company or simply taking the courage to start your own business.

The purpose of this book is to change the perspective on how to face your reality and make you understand that you are not the first to feel this way nor will they be the last, the important thing is to react and not let circumstances take control of your destiny.

Lesson 1

Frustrated with my job

Lesson 2

If you have to restart, restart!

Lesson 3

How to start a business

Lesson 4

Getting to Success

Lesson 5

Keep on the top

Lesson 6

Invest after a failure: My mistakes along the way

Lesson 7

Invest after a failure: Get up and continue

Lesson 8

Don't be afraid of risk

Lesson 1

Frustrated with my job

At some point in our lives, all of us who have ever worked for a company, feel frustrated or unhappy in our job. Those who were not born in a golden cradle necessarily must look for a job to be able to support themselves and often a family. Personally, I had a situation in the company where I worked. I remember that I had been doing the same thing for almost 3 years, I was already bored, I was on a computer all day and felt that nothing I was doing helped me to be a better professional.

One day out of nowhere, the company decided to change my boss and send me to an area where I was going to have less exposure than I already had at that moment. I remember being frustrated that day that I even wanted to be fired, but what was I going to achieve with that? I didn't have the slightest offer for a better job, so I had to "fight against my will." That day I even argued with my wife because I felt misunderstood, I even thought that I had chosen a bad career and that I would never get anywhere. How many people have reached this point of feeling misunderstood, frustrated or sad with what they do? They feel that there is no point to continue with the job, but they do not stop doing it, they really need the money. In my opinion, this is the lowest point that a person can reach in the job career, that is, working in something that they do not like because they have no other choice. Fortunately, there are people who have been through something like this and have overcome that situation. I want to mention 4 points that will help you see everything differently and that will bring out the positive from the negative.

Change your attitude. This is personally the most important step in a negative situation. We are responsible for our destiny. It is us who decide what to do with our problems, if we let ourselves die with them or if we take them as opportunities for improvement. I am a faithful believer that when things happen it is because something better will come. We must learn to understand that we must adapt to a changing world. If we lock ourselves in a negative position and say things like "*how unlucky I am*", "*I will never get anywhere*", "*everyone does well except me*", among other things, we will never really achieve something.

It is our words that tie us to a destination. It is important to maintain a positive attitude in an uncomfortable situation. We cannot blame others for our failures or try to justify why we have not got where we want, why nobody cares about us or why our bosses do not like us. Sometimes things are not going to go as we want, but if we want to get to the top, it is necessary to take a positive attitude and see what we must do to reverse the situation. We must improve our mood, refresh the mind and move forward.

Order your thoughts. This is the next step after accepting the negative situation we are in. Once we have taken an attitude of bringing out the positive in our situation, now is the time to put our thoughts on what we can do. The greatest entrepreneurs and inventors in history had many negative circumstances in their lives, but it was their positive attitude and their desire to get ahead that made them go far in life. It is time to put our thoughts in order and see where we are failing. There is no need to blame the rest, if we do not go far it is because we have not done enough to achieve it.

At this stage we analyze ourselves as individuals and see what we are good at, we see if there is any possibility of changing what we currently do and if in the future, we can work on something that we really like. In my case, I remember being frustrated working on data entry for the company. I felt that what I did at that point was unworthy since many people knew what I knew, in other words, I wasn't at all essential. I knew that I needed to differentiate myself from others. I needed to do something that not everyone knew how to do. At this point is where we must decide what we want in our lives. I had to go to the past and see why I have chosen my career, at that moment, it was when I realized that what I was currently doing was not related to what I have dreamed of doing when I was younger.

Unfortunately, no one was going to get me out of that position, everything would change if I decided to change. No one else was going to do that for me. Here we have 2 paths to take, or we decide to live our whole life regretting that we have never achieved anything, or we simply turn the page and decide to change our own destiny. If we accept the second path, I recommend any of these 2 options. Both will take you far soon. These are being a specialist or being an entrepreneur. You can even have both and get more out of it.

Specialize. Many people find it hard to start a business, most of them never achieve it. This does not mean that they will be a failure or that they will never have money. There are many cases in which people who work for a big company get to have much more money and become much happier than people who own companies. But it all lies in a simple truth: "If I want to go far, I must be different from others, if I want to go far, I must be willing to do what others do not want to do." Putted in other words, if you really want to be someone in a big company, you should seek to specialize.

When I talk about specializing, it's not just about getting a master's degree. These days, the master's degree is something common and there are very few master's degrees that really specialize in a certain topic. Personally, I think it is very good to get the master's degree, but when I say to specialize, I mean to develop yourself in something you currently do or in something you would like to do. Whether you focus on what you do or what you would like to do, you must strive as if your life depended on it. You must fall in love with the product or service that the company currently has and I am not referring to a specific brand, I am speaking of the good that the company offers. You need to specialize in it, understand where it comes from, why it is done that way, how it can be improved, what makes them different from the competition, learn how to do it yourself, among other things. Just look at the company you work for, are the people with the best jobs simple managers or experts in the area where they operate? You will realize that if you want to be in the highest positions you must learn a lot and be a specialist, know what others do not know and do what others do not.

Entrepreneurship. This was the path that I took. From a young age, I always wanted to be a business owner and have enough money for myself and my family. At that time, I realized that what I wanted was to work on something that I liked to do, owning my time and understanding that the money would come alone. I kept working where I was, but with a different attitude and focused on producing some money and then investing it in my business. I started dedicating myself completely to investing my money in my own, being my own boss. This option, in my opinion, is the one we should all aspire to as we control our time and above all, we have the freedom to make our own decisions.

If you decide to be an entrepreneur, you must know that not everything will be easy, that you will have to look for creative ideas where to invest your money. I have urged through different lessons to invest and strive to reach the top, but it is not just saying it, you must believe in it. If you want to be a great businessman, you must see what others do not see, you must be aware of new opportunities. Do not think that overnight you will have money. It will take you to a heavy road, where there will be difficulties, low income at the beginning or even tears, but if you keep the focus on what you want, the top awaits you. Don't think about taking shortcuts or investing in what others already invest on. Be creative, innovative, take an interest in others, learn to share and above all, be very determined. If you currently do not know what to invest in, you can analyze what you are good at and what you would like to do.

Once this is decided, see how you can make this a business. You will be surprised to see how by doing something you like; the money will come by itself. Something that I did, and you can use this as an example, was to buy a notebook and for each page, I started to put a business idea as a title. On each page, I defined for my ideas what was the positive and the negative of each option. After a good time thinking, I decided what were the best options to invest in. It does not necessarily have to be just an idea, it may be 2 or 3 more, but try not to be involved in everything, since as the saying goes "he who embraces much, presses little." Instead of having so many things to think about, you better focus on 2 or 3 good ideas and develop them as a business. At the time when you have the first idea developed, you can invest in new businesses.

Remember that in this life nothing is written in stone. You decide if you will go far or if you will stay in the safe zone. What I can tell you is that to be successful you must be willing to go beyond others. Don't limit yourself and don't settle for your current situation. Specialize in something you like, whether you provide your services for a big company or if you decide to invest in your own business. Accept where you are but learn to see new opportunities to be better. Before all the things, that your attitude is what defines you, as Mary Engelbreit said: "*If you don't like something, change it; if you can't change it, change the way you think about it"*.

Lesson 2

If you have to restart, restart!

I still remember the time I decided to apply for a Manager position in the company where I worked. Without fear of being wrong, each of us has always dreamed of being a company executive, and I was no exception. At that time, I was a department coordinator and my next step was that one. I felt like I was ready to take the big leap. I felt that deep down I deserved it more than anyone since I fulfilled all the requirements, but above all, I felt that my boss at that time owed me that growth.

To be honest, something inside told me that I would not be the chosen one. I even came to think of so many ways on how to reclaim my boss in case he didn't choose me, in my own perspective at that time, I was the best. I remember that the clock marked three in the afternoon. It was time for my interview, and I was prepared with everything. When I sat in my boss's office, he smiled at me and asked how I was feeling at that moment. I told him that everything was fine and that it was time for me to take that step, that I felt ready. I have in my mind the moment when he went down the printed sheets of my resume just to ask: "*Vinny, do you really want to be a manager?*". Without hesitation I answered of course, it was everything I always wanted. He asked one more question and with that my whole world changed forever. His question was, "*Vinny, what makes you think you are ready to be a Manager?*"

At that moment a great doubt entered my interior, I thought I was prepared, but deep down I was not. My boss put me through some cases to find out what I would do when making decisions and it turns out that, to my surprise, I had no idea. Many say that a person is never prepared to be a manager, and possibly it is true, but when a person really wants and can do something, they are convinced that they can achieve it. At that point in my life, I understood that I was not.

We continued with the interview, he told me that I was a well-prepared person, that I had an endless number of values that would make me a good leader, but that lately I had felt down. In all the time we worked together, he never saw in me a genuine interest in developing myself in that field. He saw that I did things because he asked me to and not because I wanted to give that extra effort. He hinted that I wanted the manager position simply to move from where I was and to stop what I was currently doing. My boss was absolutely right.

A little disappointed by the situation, I left the office straight to my desk. For a moment, I was sad to see there was my growth opportunity taken from me. After a few minutes like this, I thought I should take advantage of everything my boss made me understand that day. The last thing I occupied was feeling betrayed by him, in the end, it wasn't his fault, it was my lack of attitude that didn't allow me to prepare myself more to be the manager that the division needed at the time. At the same time something in that moment changed my perspective of things. Deep down, the reason I never gave that extra effort in that place was because inside of me, I never wanted to grow there. In the past, I had taken the job for the reason that I needed it and not because I was passionate about growing up in that company. Then I reached my break point and the only thing I could do at that moment was to <u>Restart</u>.

Don't be afraid to start from scratch. At that moment, I made the decision to see what I really wanted in my life. To think if I was willing to adapt to the fact that I liked the field where I was working in or maybe I was looking for something else. My dream was always to own my company and I felt that it was time to pursue that goal. Obviously, it was not overnight that I would be able to do it, for that I had to take the time to see where I could invest and especially how to prepare for such a challenge. I will always advise starting a business of your own, but not everyone will want that, and some people will prefer to continue in companies that can give them security.

Possibly you want to grow in these companies and develop there, but it is all a matter of attitude. No matter how prepared you are in degrees and work experiences, if there is no correct attitude, you will never be taken seriously. That was what I never had, an attitude of growing in that company and it was simply because in the bottom of my heart, I did not want to develop there. I wanted to apply for a new job, I was no longer satisfied with my position, but after some time, even if I was promoted, I would have entered a state of nonconformity again. That nonconformance was because my dream was to start a business and not to work for someone else.

This was one of the failures I had to go through in order to have enough determination to become an Entrepreneur. From this point in my life, I was already more than convinced that I should become my own boss. The question here was, when was the right time to do it. Throughout my life, small details like this made me open my eyes little by little. I had to seek new opportunities to be happy, to do something that I liked and to be paid for it.

I don't know what position you are in right now, in the end you know yourselves the best, the only thing I can tell you is to do something because you like to and because you feel you want to grow in that area and not for the money. It's hard for many people to chase a dream, perhaps they have so much to pay that they can't afford to quit a job. My advice is not that, it is not that you have to stop what you currently do and go out to seek immediately for what you want, after all, I understand that we all have responsibilities and we must fulfill them. However, you can work on what you are currently doing and gradually search opportunities somewhere else where you can feel good, whether it's founding your own business or moving to another company or division that really interests you. As the saying goes: "*Don't let go a tree branch until you have held the other*".

Don't listen to what others say. For me this is the worst mistake of the human being, seeking to get along with everyone. From the moment we try to please everyone, we will never be happy as an individual. Many people will talk and say that you are a failure and that you don't know what you want. The worst part of this is that many people push their frustrations towards you, since they have never achieved anything. This is your life, just yours. If you already have a family to take care of, good for you as you have an extra motivator. Remember, nothing you do, do it so people can see you. Try to get ahead, try to be better, so you can feel good and not because of what you project to society.

In the company where I was working, there were so many double-face people. People who on the one hand gave the impression that they were interested in you, but on the other hand were hoping that it would go badly for you. I think that this is something common everywhere. There are always people who, when they do not achieve something, they don't want anyone else to achieve it. Unfortunately, I was in a place like this and when this people realized that I had tried to be a manager and that I failed, they wanted me to see their empathy, but I knew that deep down they were glad that I continued there with them, without growing up.

At this point I realized that I couldn't go on like this. I did not want to be surrounded by this type of people, much less contaminate myself with what they were. I did not want to continue working against my will. I really had to seek to do something that I liked and so much, that the growths occurred alone. This applies both to starting our own company and to starting to work on something that we really like. Time goes by so fast and with our minds busy, that when we least expect it, we will have grown. Starting from scratch or restarting should not be a synonymous of shame.

As I have mentioned before, how many successful people have started from scratch to succeed. Shame on the day you adjust yourself to become average and let others run your life. The old saying goes: "*Success is the sum of all failures.*" Every failure is one step, we can't transport ourselves automatically to the top, things don't work like that. It is not that tomorrow someone will come and give us their company to run, or out of the nowhere someone will give us millions of dollars to start our own business. Everything is with effort, determination and hard work. If you fail along the way, get up and continue. Move forward, step by step, until you achieve what you want.

Income level does not mean greater happiness. This phrase is something that a college professor told me in my first master's classes and that I have always kept in mind. I remember telling him that I was doing my best at the company I worked for, I wanted to earn more money to have a big house and a brand-new car. He was a very nice person to talk to. He was highly trained and graduated from one of the best universities in Europe. When I told him that, he only looked at me with pitiful eyes and surely thinking inside that I was a poor naive. Honestly, I was, I had just started my 20s. I was a young man wanting to excel, but I knew nothing of the business world. That day that professor gave me a life lesson that I have always had with me since my youth.

Following the conversation with him, he asked me how I envisioned myself. I told him like a successful businessman, having everything I wanted. He told me that I had to work hard for it and above all, not to make his mistakes. I asked him why he was saying that to me, I looked at him and I saw a happy person teaching classes at night and during the day working in a multinational company. Surely, he was earning money very well. He said something to me with his heart, with a pressure on his chest: "*Vinny, just because I have money doesn't mean I'm happy. The income level of a person does not determine that they have greater happiness*".

At first, I did not understand why he was saying that to me, inside I thought how can this man tell me that? He lived in a prestigious residential in the city and had a brand-new car. He told me that in order to get there, he had to work hard and continued to do so. His life was college classes in the morning, working normal hours in the day, master classes in the evenings and to end the week, a whole Saturday teaching at another university. The man earned very well, but he was so busy all the time, that he could not enjoy what he had. I asked him why he was doing all that and he told me that he had his job at the multinational because he was paid very well, but deep down, he was not happy there.

I asked him then why he kept teaching at the university. He looked at me one more time and said something that I still have very much in mind: "*Vinny, I teach the classes at the university because it is what makes me happy, it is the part of the day where I feel that I am myself*". I understood at that point why the professor taught students. He really liked doing it. He did not want the young people to get lost and taught them things like the ones he taught me that day. He was not at all occupying that money from the university. He just did it because he had passion for it. The payment didn't matter to him anyway, that money came alone.

Perhaps at some point of his life that professor quitted his job at the multinational company to devote himself fully to teaching. How many times we do things for money? Sometimes we prefer to work in somethings that we do not want to do just for money and that's when the frustrations come and, in many times, it is difficult to reverse that situation. Sadly, we have to adapt to continue working in that place until we save enough money for a decent retirement.

I will keep repeating it always, we must do things passionately. That passion is achieved if you are happy where you are or if you do something that you really like. Whether we decide to transfer that passion to our own company or someone else's, we must be aware that our job must be something that we enjoy doing. Possibly in the beginning, the pay is not what we expect or below average compared to other fields, but in the end the money comes alone, only if we do something with passion. Having money, as the professor said, will not necessarily make us happy. When we start to do something we like, at first, we have to accept to live with what we earn at that moment, knowing that at some point, our economic situation will improve. We do not have to get the sad obsession of becoming rich doing something that we do not like.

Life will give you opportunities to grow as a person and as a professional, and that is often through failures. Things will not always go as we want, even so, we must continue to fight. The great entrepreneurs have started from scratch many times, with more desire than the previous time because they already have a knowledge that they did not have before. If you are at the moment when you still do not find the right key, keep trying that at some point you will succeed. As Steve Jobs said: "*I am not afraid to start from scratch*".

Lesson 3

How to start a business

How many times have we entered online pages that want to teach us ways to make money from home? What is funny is that it seems that all these pages copy information from each other and just change some words to give you the same exact idea. Don't get me wrong, possibly this works, but it takes more effort than you thought. For example, some blogs or online pages recommend you create your own blog, joining an affiliate market, or creating your YouTube channel, among other ideas. It sounds too simple; the problem is when we get to the starting point..."What can I talk about?". This is a problem since many people find it too difficult to be eloquent, others find it difficult to express what they feel.

In my case, writing has always fascinated me, but I know it is something that not everyone like to do. In short, creating a blog if you do not have much to write, does not seem to be the best idea. Similarly, making a YouTube channel, if you do not have the creativity to make videos, it would not be the most recommended idea. I know there are ways to trick the system, perhaps uploading other people's videos and only editing certain things so that it is not identical to others, just waiting for YouTube to pay you thousands of dollars for millions of views that will most likely never arrive. Also creating a blog with other people's writings and only editing some words, which possibly works, but in the long run it depends too much on luck and not it your effort.

There are people who are very talented earning money through the internet, but it requires patience and above all, to be clever on the web. Unfortunately, many of us do not know how to do things on the internet and that is why we have to find other ways. I am a faithful believer that we must take the noisiest rivers, because it means that not many have crossed them. You have to try to be more creative when you want to start a business. Success will arrive if it is something that we are passionate about and not for being carried away because a business worked for another person.

Following with the example of the blog, possibly that works for some people because they have a passion for writing or simply have the facility to express themselves through words and maintain the interest of their readers. That doesn't mean it works for everyone. So before starting a business, it is necessary to define what you like to do. It is not a good idea to invest in a business that you know very little about or do not like to do. A creative mind develops when it is focused on what it does. Focus on what we do is the key to success.

My wisest advice is as a first step, focus on what you want to achieve. To begin, define what things you see achieving, in how long, where you want to invest, where you want to work, etc. It is important to know what you want, there are many people who live day by day, they do not have goals, they do not have the slightest idea what they want for the future. They simply let life determine their destiny. In my case, I always wanted to be an entrepreneur, owner of my own time and my own resources. I wanted to make money work for me and without doing much effort, I could generate good amounts of money. I remember how years ago I was working for a multinational company. It was a very solid and recognized corporation, unfortunately the growth opportunities depended only on the managers on duty. Those managers on duty are sometimes hypocritical, selfish and arrogant. Sadly, the growth of people like me depended mostly on their decisions.

One of the situations that marked my life was that, in an internal change in the organization, I stopped reporting to who at the time was my boss. After 3 years, I became a complete stranger to the guy, I even applied to a position with this person, only to be told that he had chosen someone else. At some point it was my fault, I was no longer motivated of what I was doing at that time. I think in the end, that didn't work in my favor. Anyways, it is so frustrating to know that because of preferences or, as we say in my city, "by a favor", the best positions are sometimes taken in an organization by other people. No matter how much time you spent doing the best for someone, that stupid favor to others, sometimes makes other people grow before you.

That day I understood that life as an employee was not for me. I didn't want my success to depend on anyone else. Obviously, I could not resign, I was already married, and I had my first major responsibility, a house, which in the long run I understood was more a liability than an asset, since most of my income was to pay for that house, which was not generating any utility. I knew I had to keep working, but I was determined to invest. I got to the point where many of you are right now...how do you start a business? There is a key word in all of this besides passion and this is, as I mentioned earlier, to be focused.

Being focused makes us see those opportunities that no one else sees. To focus helps us seek our north. Things that we used to see as nonsense, become attractive business ideas. I'll give you my example so you can get an idea of how creating a business works, at least a profitable one. For a long time, I had an uncle who worked for a cap factory. From time to time, the factory gave him some caps to share with his family. He gave my mom a bag of them with a variety of colors, but without any logo, since this company was dedicated to selling caps to large companies at a cheap price so that they were able to stamp their brand and sell them more expensive.

For more than 5 years I received caps from my uncle frequently. Practically, I give away all of these caps to friends. I'm pretty sure that I kept less than 10 caps throughout that period, which I liked and were part of my collection. To be honest, of those 10 caps I only wore 3. All the other caps that my uncle gave us, my family and I usually gave them to other people. Even my brother was so bored with those non-branded caps, that he didn't wear any. At the time when I was determined to start my business, I saw that opportunity. It's funny to think that for more than 5 years I was receiving and giving away caps and I never saw it as a business idea. Once focused, I saw my first opportunity.

I remember telling my mom to give me the whole bag of caps my uncle gave her that month. She asked me why, since I had never proved to be a fan of those caps without designs. She only suggested not to waste them, since there were people in my grandfather's town who worked in the fields and would like to have a cap. Knowing that this was my chance to start, I grabbed the bag of caps. To be honest, there weren't many, I think the bag had by far 15 caps of different colors. I realized that the reason my family gave the caps away was because they were boring, people usually liked flashy things. I knew that if my uncle instead of these caps gave me baseball caps, I would have a collection of over 30. But since they weren't interesting, we just gave them away.

I started searching for ways on how to make cap designs. As I've said a thousand times, a focused mind does the impossible. At that time, my mother had a person who helped her with house duties. Her work time was from 8:00 am until 5:00 pm. Later she usually went to the room at the back of my parents' house. Sometimes, she stayed longer, basically when my parents left home and needed someone to take care of it. Many times, I stayed at home, I noticed that she had a particular talent for knitting. She liked to make blankets, cushions, and other things that could be woven. Knowing this, I made her a business proposal. I told her that I could give her an amount of money for each manual embroidery that she did for me.

It was all a matter of working with numbers. The caps were a gift, so I did not have to invest in raw materials. I only took up yarn and knitting needles. Obviously, I had to pay the lady for each design she made for me. I remember looking in magazines for some cool designs that could be applied to the caps. We got down to business. For each cap, I earned the triple of the regular cap cost. My job was simple, find cool designs that she could knit and voila, I already had my inventory. My next step was to sell the caps. For many people, this is the most difficult challenge. In the same way, I can tell you that being focused is also a key in this part of the process. This part requires extreme attention to see the most profitable markets.

I remember my cousin being on the school's baseball team at that time. The games were Saturday mornings, so the sun was present almost every game. I made a deal with my younger sister, who was very outgoing by the way. I told her that for every cap she sold at my cousin's games, I'd give her a well-paid commission. To my surprise, at my cousin's first game, my sister sold all the caps. There were only 15 one might say, but it gave me the guideline that things, when you put effort and dedication, work perfectly. I realized that this was my opportunity to start a business. This time I decided to talk personally with my uncle and ask him if I could buy more caps from him. He accepted with pleasure, he even gave me some caps that he already had for free and he got the other ones at discount price. Over time, I sold many caps, always using the manual embroidery technique that my mother's employee did. I had practically a small system installed that was generating an extra income to my earnings and I didn't have to make any effort. Simple, I had people making money for me.

My uncle got me the raw material at a very low price, sometimes in the form of royalties. My mom's employee was my manufacturer, since she wove the designs to the caps. On the other side my sister, since she liked to make easy money, she expanded from just selling at my cousin's games to her college. It was nice to see how such a small system was generating money to cover expenses. As I saw that it was profitable, I decided to advance to the next level. After a few months I had been able to save a little money and decided to invest in an embroidery machine. I always kept giving my mom's employee small jobs, but this time I wanted to do something more specialized. Since I already had a machine, I saw other opportunities.

I remember that one of my first sales was a batch of 30 caps to a security company that wanted their logo on them. It was a very easy sale that opened another door for me at that time. The owner of that company asked me if I could make uniforms. Seeing another opportunity in my eyes, I said yes without hesitation. I went to a store to buy local shirts and just by stamping the embroidery, I was earning more than double on each one. After just making caps, I started making uniforms and embroidery on towels as well. What was once a small business was gradually matching my current salary and without myself doing anything, just thinking.

After some years, I was making more money and investing in other businesses, including real estate. Today, the business of caps, mugs and T-shirts is possibly somehow exploited, but use this example to give you an illustration of how if we focus, we can achieve great things. Even now sales channels can be exploited in our favor through social networks, which was different a few years ago.

The biggest problem in working for others is that our mind is only focused producing for them and not for ourselves. If you are currently working for a company, take time at night to think about where you can invest. Analyze all your environment in a shopping center, supermarket, etc. See what people do and see how you could make life easier for them. There lies the key in a business, seeing the opportunities. It is important to change our mentality that we need a job or that we need money. We must go beyond that and focus on producing for ourselves. Many ideas require patience to be developed. If we don't act, life will pass us by without having done anything.

Lesson 4

John D. Rockefeller: Getting to Success

How many of us have heard about the famous businessman and billionaire John D. Rockefeller in life? At some point we have heard that name and associate it with success and wealth. This time we will talk about him and more than admire him for his wealth, we will admire him for his spirit of going beyond others and his determination to do business, even in times of crisis or recession.

There is no need to tell his story, we can easily find it on some internet site with great details. Nor will we focus on the ways in which he invested his money. However, I want to talk about 10 John D. Rockefeller Phrases that will lead you to prosperity. We will classify them in 2 stages. The first will be focused on Reaching Success and the second on Staying on the Top. As an old saying goes, "*You don't need just to get to the top, you have to stay on it*".

John D. Rockefeller was an oil businessman considered one of the richest men in all of history. Interestingly, Rockefeller was not born into a wealthy family, but rather started his path to success from scratch. It is said that his parents from a young age taught him the value of money and work. In order to go far in business and even in life, it is necessary to have order and discipline in everything we do. We'll first focus on 5 phrases Rockefeller used to reach the top.

"Don't be afraid to give up the good to go for the great". I could say that practically every individual who was not born into a wealthy family was instilled from a young age to study a college degree, in order to have a good job that would allow him to have a house and money to live in dignity. I include myself in that group in which our parents instilled in us to play it safe and study a career, trying to live debt-free in the future. The first step to success is to leave behind that idea of being an employee and becoming an entrepreneur.

Let's apply it in our lives, having a university study is good and prepares us for the future, but it should not be just that. You don't have to study to think about working for others, that should not be the idea of going to a university. If you attend university it is to acquire knowledge that allows you to be a leader and to know how to wisely invest your money. With his parent's education in order and discipline, Rockefeller applied this knowledge in business and investment.

Unfortunately, people stick to the safe, they study to have a good job with a good salary. Our idea is to save money excessively because we never learned how to invest it, basically for fear of losing it. If you want to reach prosperity you must leave that comfort you are in, otherwise your life will pass by and you will never have done anything.

"If you want to succeed you should strike out on new paths, rather than travel the worn paths of accepted success". In life, you have to do new things or take alternative paths that have not been traveled by other people. We continue with the example of a young man from the middle class who decides to attend university in search of a better future. It is perfect to finish a university career, but you must know how to manage the knowledge you acquired there.

Personally, I think it is a mistake to finish a career to get a fairly well-paid job. It is not something bad, but most people have taken this path and the negative part is that there is an increasing number of new graduates and few jobs generated in the market.

I have met many people over the age of 50, with university degrees, who are not being employed because they are not young enough. Even computers are already replacing the human being. You have to look for alternatives to new businesses or investments. Possibly you will have to start in someone else's company to earn money, I suggest that in addition to this you do it to gain experience and if possible, to save a little money and start investing in other independent businesses that will leave you an extra income. Do not settle in a company, in the end, companies take the two most important human resources, time and freedom.

"I do not think there is any other quality so essential to success of any kind as the quality of perseverance. It overcomes almost everything, even nature". Someone with perseverance insists and continues to insist until he achieves what he wants. Rockefeller was a vivid example that opportunities are taken by the risky and those who are not afraid to fail. Even if someone lacks a specific talent, with perseverance they can achieve anything over time. This virtue must go hand in hand with determination.

Without determination it is very difficult to achieve success. It is practically essential to have all the desire to reach the top. It is that passion in believing in us that makes us overcome failures and achieve what we want. If you are a person who with the first fall decides not to try it, unfortunately the top is not for you. The greatest entrepreneurs of humanity have fallen over and over again, but what makes them different from ordinary people is that they transform those failures into learning and continue their goal toward the top. They keep trying and trying until they get what they want. Don't be afraid to be wrong, the person who has not failed is because he has never tried anything. Failure is part of success, if you learn from your mistakes you will know which direction to take.

"I know of nothing more despicable and pathetic than a man who devotes all the hours of the waking day to the making of money for money's sake". Putted in other words, wage labor does not give time to generate money. Sometimes people are more focused in generating money for others than in generating for themselves. Unfortunately, most people have fallen and will continue to fall into this error. That's what makes the difference between employee and employer.

The employee works for others while the employer makes other people work for him. Someone who works all day has no time to think. A busy mind on a workday has little time to see opportunities or ways to invest money. The saddest thing in life is that many people who gave their lives for a company, end up being just one more number for this one. I do not know of any case in which the owner of a company decides to give part of his fortune to an employee for being good.

In this life, each one creates his own destiny, you decide if you invest it in generating for yourself or generating for others. Time is one of the best assets of people. Use your time wisely and what better way to generate income for you and your family. If you already work as an employee, you don't need to quit today. Good decisions are not made on impulse. I simply suggest that you go looking at ways in which you can invest the money that you generate currently working. There are many people who say: "*The money I earn is not enough,*" "*When I earn more money, I will invest,*" "*Right now, I have other priorities.*" Unfortunately, these people never succeed.

If you want to reach the top you must fight for it. You don't need to have money to invest. It is simply to think and analyze where the opportunities are. There are so many cases of people that using the money of others reached the top. Think about how to invest your money and if you have so little, look for how to invest money of others.

"If your only goal is to become rich, you will never achieve it". Don't work to make money. Becoming rich should not be your main goal in life, but rather the consequence of having done something good. Rockefeller mentioned that if your goal is just that, you will never achieve it. Wealth comes to you when you do something that benefits others, be it a quality product or service. You must believe in what you do so that others also believe in you.

There are people who say that there is nothing more beautiful than making money doing what you like. When your mind is focused on doing something you are good at, you spend time and effort on it. If you have a product or service, when you offer it, pretend this was for you. You will realize that little by little you will earn money without looking for it. There is nothing worse than a person who is obsessed with making money. His ideas are not correct, he invests in things he does not know, simply just because others did well. They are selfish, greedy people and do not help others. They are so focused on making money that they forget how they treat people. In the end, people are the ones who give you their money in exchange for your product or service.

If you don't know what you're good at, you can talk to people in your circle and see what your skills and strengths are. If you find the answer, try turning it into a business. Success is not easy, it requires a lot of effort and above all perseverance. It is your decision whether to let time go by doing what you currently do without making a change in your life. I can only tell you, don't expect to be successful if you don't do your part, as Albert Einstein said: "*Insanity is doing the same thing over and over again and expecting different results.*" In our next topic we will continue with Rockefeller phrases but this time to stay on the top. And remember, only you are responsible for your destiny, as William Ernest Henley said: "*I am the master of my fate: I am the captain of my soul*".

Lesson 5

John D. Rockefeller: Keep on the top

Following with the previous topic, we will talk about the other 5 Rockefeller phrases for prosperity, but this time oriented to how once we have achieved success, stay on the top.

Rockefeller at a young age understood that to be prosperous it is necessary to do what others do not. In his childhood, Rockefeller collected stones that he then painted and sold to his classmates. From what was generated, he got his first savings. It is said that soon after, a friend of his father borrowed money from him but on the condition that he return it with an annual interest. At the time, this person did his part. Having the money back with interest, Rockefeller realized that the money should work for him and not the other way around.

"I would rather earn 1% off 100 people's efforts than 100% of my own efforts". What Rockefeller does is compare the income of an employer with multiple employees against the income of a common worker. His motto was that he preferred to use the effort of other people, being able to take advantage of their knowledge, time and performance factor and not only work for a salary.

Rockefeller preferred to give jobs to several people and earn 1% of their capacity instead of working himself 100% of his own efforts, in the end, the return he would get doing things alone was less. With that, he made the money work for him, giving more people jobs and achieving a percentage of profit.

There are many ways of doing business that do not necessarily require all your effort to get done. You can even have other people do it for you and only take a percentage of the profit. The problem for many is that they want the biggest piece of the pie and cannot make others feel happy working with them. They focus more on making money than on thinking about how to make a business sustainable. It is unnecessary to want to get rich in a single business when you can have several that, little by little, will generate more. You must keep a balance.

You can invest in several businesses but be fair to the people who work for you, so that you can achieve their commitment. Learn to work with others so that your mind is clearer when it comes to making decisions and when it comes to new investments.

"The way to make money is to buy when blood is running in the streets". It sounds more crazy or scary than what it really means. Whether it's fact or fiction, Rockefeller is said to read the newspaper every morning in a park while someone cleaned his shoes. He liked to talk about any topic with them. Once, one of these shoeshine boys out of nowhere started talking about economics and investing in the stock market. It is at that moment that Rockefeller decides to sell everything. This has nothing but a simple meaning, buy in panic and sell in euphoria.

What Rockefeller did was sell his stocks when everyone was investing in a certain market and buy when everyone was afraid to do so. What Rockefeller hinted is that you shouldn't look for businesses where everyone is looking to invest, or simply because someone else has done well. You must go beyond others, take those opportunities that no one has taken and turn it into a business. Many will say that it is more difficult than it seems, but if you do not think and analyze where you could apply your strengths, your economic situation will hardly change.

You have to be clear about something, nobody in this life will give you anything, so do not expect to find where to invest on the internet because nobody will give you their formula for doing business. If you really want to start a successful business, you must work hard to see where it is worth investing. No successful entrepreneur will make it easy for you, so if you want to be one, don't expect someone to facilitate things.

"The only question with wealth is, what do you do with it?" This happens when you start earning money. Many might wonder, "*Now that I have money, what can I do with it?*" Personally, I like to classify people who manage to make some money into 3 types: People who live to survive, People who live for others to see and People who live to enjoy.

The person who lives to survive is the common person, in other words, the employee who lives day by day thinking about how to spend their money on liabilities. These people have a regular salary but are focused only on expenses that leave them no income. Many of these people come to have the possibility of saving and investing, but instead they prefer to buy a newer car, a better television, etc. They use their money only to spend it, complaining about not having so at the end of each month. They do not make the slightest effort to have a fund to save or invest.

The person who lives for others to see is someone who already earns better than average. In this group we can include professionals with a very good income but who are more focused on their profile. They are people who like to indulge themselves just so that others can see that they are on the top. This is what we mean by people who pay large amounts of money on trips, buy houses in places with the highest mortgage rates, keep their credit cards full and attend the finest restaurants, among other things. I like to call this group "Selfie Dudes". They are people who get to earn good amounts of money, but their lifestyle makes them not save or save the least possible. Most of them, when time has passed by, lose everything since they did not take advantage of their wealthy time.

The person who lives to enjoy is in short, the rich person. A truly wealthy person understands the rules of money, income control, and expense control. People who don't know about money management will quickly lose it. It is not a bad thing to indulge yourself once in a while, if life is to be enjoyed altogether, but you must control what comes out of your bag, in other words, you must know what stage of your life you are at. Unlike the other types of people, the really rich convert their income into assets, they invest their money in businesses that can produce more money for them. They don't care what others think about their appearance, they are more focused on producing and investing. Many people think that you must have money from a young age to be able to be rich. If a person wants to belong to this group, they must first save some money, then acquire investment in business knowledge, and then see where to invest for more profits. Even with low incomes, money can be converted into assets, into independent incomes, whether we work for a company or not.

"It is wrong to assume that men of immense wealth are always happy". One of the biggest mistakes a man could make is to catalog another person by his economic status and not by his human quality. There are people who get to have so much money that it becomes their best friend. They focus so much on being rich that they forget about others. There is no use of having a fortune if you do not have your loved ones by your side. Don't be obsessed with being rich because you will never make it and if you make it, you will have separated those who love you along the way. There is no person richer than someone who has family and friends. If you strike a balance between having money and growing your family, you will realize that everything will have been worth it.

More than being rich aspire to be a leader, more than being rich aspire to be an entrepreneur and more than being rich learn to be an excellent human being. This is something that the greatest entrepreneurs in the world have. They make billions of dollars, but their advantage is not in making money. They know what their customers want, they know how to lead their teams, creating their products and services in the best way at a fair price. You will be happy if by doing what you like you can make life happier for others.

"Giving should be entered into in just the same way as investing. Giving is investing". The basic rule of life is, what you sow, you reap. If you give love you receive love. If you give respect you receive respect and if you give money you receive money. Don't think you should produce just for yourself. It is important to take care of money and see where to save, but the worst mistake that a human being can make is to become someone greedy focused on their own benefit. When we say that you have to save, it does not mean that you have to save everything. If you are someone who likes to control your spending, allocate an amount of what you earn to help others. You can start by helping your family, a friend or someone in need. Do it without expecting anything in return. Just keep in mind that if you do good in the future someone else will do good with you.

If you already have your company or if in the future you manage to have one, be grateful to the people who work for you. Don't treat them like they owe you something, on the contrary, always thank them for anything they do for you. Do not be arrogant and even though you are the one who pays them, learn to be grateful, either in words or in any detail. Remember that they are your team who give you that leverage to take your business to the top.

If you ever make it to the top, always keep your feet on the ground. Be wise with how you invest your money and always seek to be one step ahead of others. But above all, be kind and generous with those around you so that they are always grateful to you. As Dale Carnegie once said: "*Giving and giving more is the only way to have more and more*".

Lesson 6

Invest after a failure: My mistakes along the way

Not everything in life is like roses. Success is not always achieved the first time. I had to make mistakes in order to be successful. I even had to fail in a business to learn. It is for this reason that I will tell you about my greatest learning and that took me to make better business decisions in the future.

There is no worse feeling for the human being than the feeling of helplessness after failure. Knowing that you want to achieve success and seeing that it is not your destiny. Doubts enter your mind and you begin to ask yourself -*Is it that I will never become a successful businessman? Could it be that I better stay working for a company where my income is secured?* The mind in those moments can become our best ally or our worst enemy. We all have to live a moment in our lives when we can decide to start again or just throw in the towel. I will tell you about my case and I hope it can help you not to make my same mistakes.

Since I was a little boy my dream was to be a great businessman. I always wanted to be able to lead many people, own my time and also have a lot of money. I mean, who in his life has not wanted this. Unfortunately, I was not born in a privileged home. My dad had a hard time giving us an education. We were a family of 4 brothers. My dad was the only source of income in the house. It was difficult in my childhood and part of my youth to see how my father sacrificed many things to give us everything. I will be infinitely grateful to him because my education was good, and I was able to graduate from college with effort. For this reason, I always had in mind to get my family ahead, it was the fuel in my blood that made me want to become a millionaire businessman and give back to my parents everything they gave me. That was always my biggest motivation.

Once graduated from university, I decided to work for a multinational company. At first it went very well, I earned more than the average of recent university graduates, I was just 20 years old and I had no commitments, so I could do with my money what I wanted. Even earning well, I felt that something was missing. I hated having to report to someone all the time for money. After 2 years in the company, I decided to invest in a business. It was kind of crazy to be honest since I was just 22 years old, but I was ready to gobble up the world. I knew that I did not have enough knowledge in something to undertake, but I could use my father's experience in the field that he had already developed. My father worked more than 30 years in the automotive industry, he was a walking bookstore on cars and their parts. He was already a manager of an auto parts company when he decided to resign and start with me. Both father and son started an adventure, at first it sounded like our rocket to the moon, but it just became our greatest learning. For this reason, I want to continue telling you my story, but I will highlight my mistakes so that you do not make them.

Invest without having financial support. We started our business with an immense desire to be the strongest company in my city. We knew that we had a lot of competition, we had to differentiate ourselves from others in order to achieve success. Taking advantage of the contacts that my father made through the years, we managed to do business with companies in other countries so that they could sell us their product and thus we could sell at a lower price in the market. We became importers of auto accessories, starting the business with the benefits obtained by resigning. We decided to rent a place to store our product. Everything was walking, unfortunately we were very poorly advised. At this stage, we made our first mistake that would later invoice us. We decided to invest all our money in the business. We had no savings and we decided to depend on the business to earn a salary.

There is an old saying that says, "*Don't put your eggs in the same basket.*" We blindly believed that our company was going to take off and that we did not need the support of a bank to get ahead. There is no bigger mistake than thinking that. Absolutely every company, whether large or small, needs a bank or credit support in order to grow. It is a basic rule of thumb in finance. You can search in a financial book or on the internet, it is necessary to request loans when investing. You will be surprised to see that there are times when it is better to invest with the money of some financial entity than with your own money. Similarly, in future books we will address this topic to explain how it works. For now, we will continue with our story...

Not knowing the environment where your business is developed. This is where our first mistake took its toll on us. When I tell you that all our money was in the business, it is because we did not have the least bit saved, everything was invested. We were so blinded that the business was good that we decided not to prepare in case something went wrong. Unfortunately, when you have your eggs in the same basket, the moment may come when you can lose everything.

On a Monday morning, we arrived with my father at the store to start a new week. When we were about to open the doors, we noticed that the main padlock had a broken key inside. We thought it was weird and we just thought it was a bad joke. I asked a neighbor for pliers so I could break the lock. When I went to return it and came back to the store, I saw the expression on my father's face. He told me the phrase that marked my life forever: *"Son, we have been robbed!"* The thieves had managed to open a wall from the store next door and ransacked the entire establishment over the weekend. They stole everything from us, they left us only a coolant that was too heavy to carry. I felt that day, in addition to losing all our investment, that I lost the desire to move on. So much effort and so much money invested lost like that out of nowhere. My mind was so blank that I just wanted to get away from my country. We lost all our money, we no longer had jobs and we still had a debt to cover with a supplier. Where do you get the desire to invest when a dream was stolen from you? How do you tell yourself that everything will be fine when everything is wrong?

Now that I am in a much better stage, I can tell you that before starting a business, as much promising it may be, you should know your environment. That was our second mistake, not analyzing the country situation, not knowing the neighborhood where we put our store, and not seeing what external threats we had.

Make decisions due to economic pressure.
Without fear of being wrong, it was the most bitter day of my life. I cried like a child. I felt that there were my dreams and my goals. The worst thing of all is that I had my father by my side suffering with me, when my only intention with this was to be able to repay what he gave me in his life and instead I managed to give him a greater misfortune. It is difficult to get up after such a blow but if we did not, my mother and my brothers would also be affected. You had to turn the page yes or yes. We decided to continue with the business, obviously beaten.

As we had no financial support, we decided to apply for loans from the companies with which we already did business. Some lent us and others did not. Unfortunately, we had debts and depended on the business to have a salary and above all, a family to feed. The business was not bad, on the contrary, it left us profits, but we were so immersed in the mud that it would be too difficult to get out. Everything was like a snowball of bad decisions. Our next mistake was to make an important decision when you're in debt.

Some people say that a big mistake is making decisions in a moment of anger or making promises in a moment of happiness. I would add something else, there are no decisions to make when you are in debt. If you have to decide something, you better take advice from people who are better than you. The funny thing is that we did seek advice from a successful businessman. We told him our idea of selling our house to invest in the business and recover the initial investment. He told us not to sell our house. Unfortunately, we were so blinded that our business would be fruitful that we decided to sell our house anyways. As you are reading it, we decided to invest the last thing we had as a family to invest in our business. How I wish I could turn back time and make myself see that it was a lethal mistake that we were making.

There are people who mortgage their home to invest in their business. Sometimes it works and others it doesn't. After so many years, I understood that this only works when they already have a system working and have a practically well-established business. All they need is a little capital. The thing is, we were just starting, we didn't have a business already running, we just ventured into the sea without paddles.

Not knowing at what stage a business is in. My grandfather used to tell me when I was a child that there is nothing worse than someone fool. We became so foolish with our business, but now I understand that it was not so much foolishness, but rather that determination to get ahead. It is positive to be determined but you must do it with open eyes, seeing in what you are trying to insist. We wanted to make the business work by force. We sold our house and again made the same mistake, we put all our investment back into the business. Inadvertently, we got carried away by the emotion that we already had capital to invest. We continue to believe that we did not need a bank to get ahead. We made the same mistake twice in putting all our investment in one basket and in not having a bank backup.

We managed to change our store's address and buy more merchandise to be able to invest. Anyone would say this is the takeoff of this company. Unfortunately, this was not the case and in time we would realize it. I like to compare a business with a tree. When a seed becomes a plant, you realize that it is growing though it is not yet big enough to sit on a branch. The same thing happens in a business. There are times when the business will grow due to the multiplying nature of things, but that doesn't mean we can already depend on it. That was our next mistake. We did not know how to interpret what stage of life our business was in. We began to collect back wages, to make our store more aesthetically beautiful, when it was a simple warehouse. In short, we wanted to give our business the appearance of a leafy tree when it was just a small growing plant.

Depend on a growing business. At that point, we used the business to pay our debts and to collect our wages. In other words, any profit was not reinvested, on the contrary, it was used to pay off debts and to pay us for our job. That was our next mistake, we cut growth on our plant. Possibly our business could have borne fruit, unfortunately we had no financial support with which to sustain ourselves and practically our small plant supported my expenses, my father's, those of my family and the general business expenses. I have used the word unfortunately in this lesson, but yes, it is a shame for me to have made all these painful mistakes, but luckily you can avoid them.

To put all the unnecessary expenses in a small business is to remove its development. Now I believe faithfully that the best way to invest is to have a backing aside, that is to say, a good saving or a primary job that allows the business to grow without making expenses other than operating the business.

Not working hard enough to grow the business. If you don't make the greatest effort to achieve something, you better not do it. If you are not willing to suffer to grow a business, you better not have it. In the end, this was our last mistake before we closed our business forever. Painful as it sounds, that was our reality. The business eventually entered a stage of depending on my father's state of mind. He was basically in charge of doing the business with customers and I was in charge of all the administration of it. The business was very exhausting through the almost three years that we had it. It was more of a burden than an investment. The fault was ours alone, for making so many mistakes.

There were days when my father was so depressed that he didn't go out at all to do business. Those were wasted days for selling. There were some other days when he did not sell anything, and it was another day without incomes. In the end of every month, the expenses were there and the incomes less and less, until we reached the point where we sat down with my dad to discuss what we should do, the situation was unsustainable. We understood that to grow a business it is necessary to have the willpower, the courage and the lucidity of mind to carry it until it sustains you at some point. Unfortunately, neither of us had the desire to continue, so we decided for our well-being and our family's, sell what we had and close our business once and for all.

Not everything in this life is a fairy tale and all great entrepreneurs do not always do well on their first try, but this is where the difference is. The successful man turns failure into learning, while the person who does not, lives regretting the mistakes made all his life. My father stayed in a smaller, separate business that allowed him to be safe. On my side, I made the decision to return to work for a multinational, I was still young.

To be honest, after that failure being an entrepreneur, I thought that my life would be to work for a company and live from it, but I did not count that life would give me more opportunities to start all over again. Things happen for a reason and all these lessons learned made me not make the same mistakes in the future. Years later, I was able to work and earn well, creating some businesses that little by little were growing and did not require me to cut their growth. In our next lesson we will be focusing, based on these errors, on being able to do the opposite and grow a business. We may have to fail at some point, but that's where you get the strength to take the next step. As Paulo Coelho mentioned: "*Failure is part of life; if you don't fail you don't learn and if you don't learn you don't change*".

Lesson 7

Invest after a failure: Get up and continue

Following with the previous lesson, our mistakes give us a better perspective on how to behave in the future. It is not easy for anyone to fail, I think that nobody wants that in life. However, it is necessary to succeed every test on the way to reach your goals. I remember once talking to a friend who was a very successful businessman by the way. I asked him how he had managed to create such a solid and fruitful company. He just laughed and said something that I will never forget: "*You are seeing my tip of the iceberg, but you have not seen everything that is under water.*" What my friend was referring to is that I only managed to see the successes that he had, however I was not able to see his frustrations, his failures, his helplessness and his saddest moments. That's the truth, every successful businessman had to go through a difficult time in his life, call it failure or call it impotence, in the end, they never gave up and achieved success.

For this reason, I want to help you with these advices that, after a big failure, helped me see business differently. I can only tell you that there may be new adversities in your lives that I may not have suffered, but you will need to face them and learn from them to continue until you are that successful businessman.

Always have financial support. If your decision in life is to be an entrepreneur, all I can do is congratulate you for your determination. Now, you have to understand that you should take advice from people who have already crossed that path, please try not to invent the whole process. Throughout my years of experience and study, I have managed to break a paradigm that I had all my youth. My parents always taught me that I should earn and save and just then, invest what I had. That statement sounds very interesting and I think several people get to achieve something by doing that. Now comes my question: Do you have enough time to save and create a large business? I think 80% of those who are reading this will never have the time to save enough to have a large company. We have so many expenses in our lives that we can save the least. You don't need to save those large amounts to be able to invest. Don't get me wrong, I'm not saying it's not good to have good savings. Save and have it as a backup against adversities, but that all your savings are not used 100% in your investment. It was useless for me to save enough money to invest everything in my business, in the end, I lost everything and did not have a backup to get up correctly.

What I want to imply is that your savings do not become the backbone of your new business. The amount of money you have saved is not what determines the size of your project. There are so many cases of people who have managed to become billionaires using the money of others. It is easier than you think. There are already forms on the internet or there are even seminars at universities that allow you to know the profitability of a business. They all seek to measure the risk of a project, to see how much time it would take to recover our investment and something that is very important, to see if it is convenient to get into debt in a bank or invest the money ourselves. It is only necessary to search a little on the subject. On the internet you can see options of "How to measure profitability in my business" or "When it is convenient for me to apply for a loan for my business".

I have a simple equation to see the impact of financial support:

% Savings + % Loan = Profitability in the business.

The proportion of each is determined with an analysis of the profitability of your business. I want you to understand that there are businesses in which it is more profitable to use 30% of own capital and 70% of the bank. There are even cases where less than that. There are cases in which using 100% of your savings to invest does not make the business profitable. The concepts of bank interest rates and the rate of own capital enter this game, but I do not want to expand on this topic because you can easily read about it on the internet. The advice that I can give you according to my experience is to save as much as you can but just to be a backup for you in hard times. You can use a part of this fund to invest it, but first do a profitability analysis of any idea you have to see how much of your savings you can invest without necessarily being at zero. I have known so many business cases that only good intentions remain. The funny thing is that many of them were good, but their founders did not have the slightest knowledge of finance. You do not need to be a financier, but you must know the basics to better understand your business.

I could easily say things like "*Don't be afraid*", "*Invest your money, that is the best*", "*You only need yourself*". All of these things are valid, but business is done with a cold head and not with feelings. You must understand that great entrepreneurs have a great knowledge of finance. At some point they created a product or service that was very good, but it was the wise use of finances that made them multiply their money.

Analyze the internal and external aspects of my business. I have heard countless times the saying: "*Let's start a business.*" Three words so simple but that putting them into practice requires more sacrifice than imagined. It is not only to fight for it, you must know a bit of finance as mentioned in the previous point and know everything about your business. When I say everything, it is not just saying I am going to buy this to sell it a little more expensive, it is to see everything that includes starting a business. In my previous lesson, I assure you that what I sold was good, my product satisfied the customer and I gave it at a relatively low price, but in my immaturity, I thought that it was only this that would lead me to success. Everyone who enters university at some point of their career is taught the term SWOT ANALYSIS (Strengths, Opportunities, Weaknesses and Threats). It sounds like a lie, but it is important to apply before starting a business. An analysis of this is essential. As in the previous point, I will not elaborate on the SWOT because you can easily read about it on the internet.

This analysis allows you to see things with a cold head in a global aspect. What can affect you within the business, and what can externally impede your growth. In my case, my country's situation was not the most optimal for investing at that time. Crime had peaked and extortion was the order of the day. To top off, what seemed like a bargain in terms of a warehouse lease price, it turned out to be the biggest blow to my business. To spend less on a store, I decided to rent it in an area with little security in the city and suffer the theft of all my investment. Possibly the circumstances with you are different, but it is necessary to evaluate your business through a SWOT to make the wisest decisions. You will see in time that all will have been worth it.

Make decisions without pressure and without feelings. The first two points are the success for any large company. Knowing the strengths and weaknesses of your company and your product or service and having a good financial knowledge, will make you reach the top faster than expected. However, even achieving the mentioned points, it is necessary to learn to make decisions. Many of us had to make decisions under economic pressure and unfortunately, they were not the most successful.

I hope that when you embark on your path to prosperity in your business, you will quickly correct the mistakes that come along the way. Possibly some people manage to build a business with minimal effort, but in most cases, this is not what happens. Most people find it very difficult to become successful in business. It is the decisions that set the course for a company. If you are already investing in your business or if one day you do, you will have to make momentous decisions. You will not be able to avoid this, since your business will depend on it.

However, you can take two simple tips that have helped me make decisions, both in my personal life and in relation to a business:

1. If you are going to make an important decision, ask for advice. The advice should be from someone who is better than you or who has accomplished something in life. People have a lot of advice to offer, but you have to look at where that advice comes from. I know that many will do it with good intentions, unfortunately, not all the advice they give you is good. To find out which ones you might listen to, just look who's coming, someone who accomplished a lot, or someone who has never done anything.
2. Never make an angry, excited, or pressured decision. Decisions are made with sufficient mental alertness to make them right. If you're about to make an important decision, try to shake off the pressure a bit. Do something you like to do, go out to eat at a restaurant, surround yourself with your friends. When you are relaxed start thinking, you will see that it is better to decide like this.

Be aware that a business is a step by step. Everything good in life requires patience. If success was so quick and easy, everyone would have it. Patience and perseverance are two of the best virtues that a successful entrepreneur can have. Many undertake the path, and some manage to last in it, however, most of the people allow themselves to be overcome by fatigue, disappointment and loss. They cannot continue even when they are close to seeing the profitability of the business. I think that every human being would like to earn money quickly, sadly at first it is never like that. You have to know that for a business to start making quick profits, it must have a good foundation, and to have this good foundation, you have to have enough patience to see the business grow.

One step at a time is knowing that sales may be quite low at first, production may be too slow, or the business simply has no form. In order to overcome this barrier, it is necessary to see the mistakes that will be made to improve them. If we cannot take advantage of mistakes to improve our company, hardly anyone will help us improve.

My grandfather used to tell me "*The greatest learning that a person can have is the learning of life. There are many people who can graduate and specialize in different fields, but it is the university of life that really teaches you.*" This applies to business in the same way. If you want to have a successful company you must learn from the mistakes you make in them, you must learn what is best for your business and what is not, what are the best practices to achieve greater profitability. Only by living your business day by day you can get the most out of it. The reason why some people run a business and others do not, is that those who excel had the patience to learn how to improve their product and make a profit from them, in the end the shortcuts are not good.

Work hard to grow the business. I like to emphasize this to the point of exhaustion. Nothing in this life is free. Nobody will give you their formula for doing business. If you want to have a successful company, you must work hard for it. You can find good advice or even best practices from other companies, but the essence of a business will have to be manufactured by yourself. I like to think that each one as an individual is responsible for his own destiny. Positioned in the market, each captain is responsible for his ship.

Both you as a leader or those who work for you must go out of their way for your company. It doesn't matter that you have to pay them more for their performance, the important thing is that your business runs at its highest capacity. You must bet to push your capacity to the limit and keep all your efforts focused on growing your business.

Lesson 8

Don't be afraid of risk

More than once we have heard the phrase "*The person who does not risk, does not win.*" Easy to say, but when the time comes to put it into practice, everyone's legs tremble. I think the reason why many do not take risks is because the fear of losing is greater than the desire to succeed. Losing money, knowing how much it has cost us to earn it, blinds us and makes us want to take maximum care of it. Without a doubt, that is one of the worst mistakes of the human being, love and fear of money. Many people live their entire lives earning and spending money. The little they manage to save, they take care of in an overprotective way, that they finally lose the meaning of life.

Life, in the material world, is easy to understand how it works. You must produce in order to enjoy and you must also learn to give to others, because the more you give, the more you receive. The problem is that more than 80% of the world population works to pay expenses, sometimes they can afford one or another luxury, but they are so tied up in debts that they rarely share with others.

If we are caught in this circle of debts, in which we take care of money more and more, it is necessary to change our way of thinking. It must be clear that, in order to be financially free, our income column must be much larger than the expense column. In order to share with others without regrets, it is necessary to have where to share. With a regular job it is very difficult to achieve financial freedom. This is because working life has an established pattern of conduct. The more you grow in a job or the more you earn at the salary level, the more you spend. It is the typical behavior of the average person. If they have a new position and are paid better, they decide to buy a better car or invest in a bigger house. This means that their debt level grows and grows and never stops, everything is expense.

For this reason, I like to highlight the fact that it is so important to invest in different businesses. It is incredible the number of people who say to me "*Vinny, I cannot invest because I do not have money.*" Every time I hear that phrase, I feel so sorry because I understand that these people will hardly be financially free. Investing does not require having large amounts of money, the key is to simply have the desire to succeed. I have always liked surrounding myself with people more successful or smarter than me. I like to listen to their experiences and see how I can apply them in my life.

This time I want to share the case of my friend James. James came from a humble family. His father was a builder and his mother worked on the cleaning equipment in a city hotel. With the effort of his family, James was able to finish school. He got to the point of going to college. Unfortunately, his parents could not afford his studies, so James had to start working when he was a recently graduated student. He mentioned that he started working with his father on construction. His father, who was already a supervisor in construction projects, paid him to help the carpenter. James took advantage of those 2 years of his life to understand the whole process of carpentry. At the end of that period, James' father became sick and the doctor recommended that he stop all construction activities, because his lungs were so contaminated with dust, that he needed to get away from it. It was a hard blow for James, as you can imagine, his father did not have money to continue supporting his mother and his siblings.

With the little they saved, his parents were able to finish paying for the house and hoped that James and his older brother would contribute with something to the house. James decided to seek for a job at a local hardware store. Having experience in wood, he was quickly entered into the wood products department. He worked Monday through Saturday, as he was part of the retail sales support team. In the evenings, on weekdays he took 2 classes at college. In the first 3 years he was only able to pass 15 classes. They were very few considering that the engineering career was somehow long. Besides this, we must add that his scores were not too good, since he rarely had time to study or do homework. James was immersed in a lifeless world. He lived to work and pay his family's expenses. He did not have time to study and much less to rest. His life was working without rest to earn a misery.

James was 21 at that time. Most of his first classmates were about to graduate from college, others already had better-paying jobs. One day, helpless with the situation in which he lived, James decided to leave college. He could no longer continue like this, he took time at night to put his thoughts in order for someday to quit that job that was very heavy and very poorly paid. James continued working for a while in the hardware store, but now, he was too determined to change the financial situation of him and his family.

He knew that in order to live better, he had to have his own business. The question was... *where to start?* James decided to focus his thoughts on where he could have other extra income aside from his salary. He noticed that in the hardware store there were pieces of wood that was just a waste of the cut. He remembered that he had learned how to work with wood. At the end of the day, with the manager's authorization, James collected this wood and took it home. In the evenings, using some tools his father had, he began making bathroom shelves. He worked so hard at making these shelves that his father helped him sell some of them with friends. They were a sensation since the shelves were inexpensive and very pretty. Little by little he was innovating in his creations, they were not only bathroom shelves, but also shelves for living rooms, kitchens and even garden areas. In a period of time, James was taking advantage of the waste of a hardware store, to generate some money. He saw that there was a market, since people liked wooden things.

With the money he collected from his sales, he decided to invest in new tools and to buy better quality material. His free time in the evenings and weekends was dedicated to make fine pieces of wood for home. One day he decided to make an offer to the owner of the hardware store to allocate his product. Seeing that the cost was low, the owner decided to give it a try. Over time, James' product was one of the most commercialized in the hardware store. At that time a problem arose, James' production capacity was not the best, since he was only making the shelves and other furniture. The demand was far greater than the supply he could give. He entered in a debate of resigning and dedicating fully to his small business or whether to continue working in the hardware store. The situation with the hardware store was that James obtained waste at no cost and had a discount on some pieces of better quality for being an employee. In the same way, he had won the owner's sympathy for his entrepreneurial spirit and because he was selling high quality product at a low cost.

Because James knew that his dedication to a perfect wooden finish made a difference, he decided to hire a carpenter to do the job of cutting and polishing the wood in the dimensions James requested. This would allow James to come home at night and on weekends, only to devote himself to the perfect finishing of his shelves and furniture. His production capacity had grown, and he could already offer more than double in furniture he previously offered. The problem came when the owner of the hardware store had recommended James' furniture to his brother, who also owned another one. James no longer had the ability to be working for the hardware store, so he decided to quit. This time he would be fully involved in the process. Demand grew not only in this new hardware store, but in other stores that James' father had managed to allocate product. Little by little, he stopped selling just in the city, he was now selling in other hardware stores along other cities of the state. In 3 years with his business, James had managed to earn much more money than he would have done in 20 years working with the hardware store.

With the demand, the need to hire more carpenters grew. James had delegated the finishing function to people he trusted. In 5 years, James had his own company with 15 employees working for him. In the next few years he would become the owner of some small loggers. Today, James is one of the most prosperous and successful entrepreneurs I have ever met. Everything was born with the mentality of being a millionaire. It all started with the desire to be prosperous and the right attitude that, if you set your mind to something, you can do it. I love this story, and whenever I can I seek to share it with people who are fearful minded.

I want you to see the case of James, who without having money to invest managed to create a great company and become a millionaire. It was all based on his dedication, his passion and his focus. Similarly, I have seen many cases of people who start generating money in a business and then move on to another that generates much more. The important thing is to start. Possibly your idea at the moment is to make homemade bread, to give you an example. It may not be a very lucrative business, but it will allow you to generate some extra money and then invest in another type of business.

Many people do not take the risk of investing simply because they are afraid of losing money that with hard work it cost them to achieve. For this reason, I give you this suggestion. Keep working at the companies where you currently work but start thinking how you could make extra money. Whatever you invest in the future, it will hurt you much less to risk that extra money. I like a phrase that the best basketball player of all time, Michael Jordan, immortalized. Michael once said, "*I can accept failure, everyone fails at something. But I can't accept not trying*".

There lies the success, in overcoming that fear of failure. If we don't try, we will never know how far we can go. Just like Jordan says, everyone fails on occasion. If this business you want to start does not work for you, it is an opportunity to grow. You may properly say that you have tried in that area, but it just didn't work.

Life is too short to let go without having done anything. The world's great and wealthy entrepreneurs more than once failed in certain business, but they persevered until they became what they are today. Nobody likes to lose money, but if we manage it safely and without risk, we will have earned too little. In order to earn money, you have to risk money. As simple as that. If your money is already committed to something else, find a way to generate the first pennies and then invest in another business with more income. The world is constantly developing, there are more and more opportunities to become a millionaire. It is all a matter of focusing and taking risks. Taking risks is for the brave. The brave is the person who goes the furthest in anything he undertakes. As Facebook founder Mark Zuckerberg says: "*The biggest risk is not taking any risk... In a world that is changing really quickly, the only strategy that is guaranteed to fail is not taking risks.*"

www.ingramcontent.com/pod-product-compliance
Lightning Source LLC
Chambersburg PA
CBHW070309220526
45465CB00004B/1814